Management Rules

50 New Rules for Managers

Jo Owen

CAPSTONE

This edition first published 2011
© 2011 Jo Owen

Registered office
Capstone Publishing Ltd. (A Wiley Company), The Atrium, Southern
Gate, Chichester, West Sussex, PO19 8SQ, United Kingdom

For details of our global editorial offices, for customer services and for
information about how to apply for permission to reuse the copyright
material in this book please see our website at www.wiley.com.

Library of Congress Cataloguing-in-Publication Data
••

A catalogue record for this book is available from the British Library.

9780857082213 (*paperback*)   9780857082473 (epdf)
9780857082480 (epub)   9780857082447 (emobi)

Set in   dia Limited

Printed   dstow,
Cornw

Illustra

CONTENTS

INTRODUCTION: MANAGEMENT RULES

Times have changed, and management has changed. Managers are having to learn new rules of survival and success. Expectations are not getting lower: they are rising all the time. Management is not becoming simpler, it is becoming harder. But for successful managers, it is also becoming more rewarding, personally and professionally.

In the past, managers made things happen through people they controlled: now managers have to make things happen through people they may not control. That changes everything.

The old world was straightforward. The bosses had the brains and the workers had the hands. Workers were not meant to do too much thinking for themselves: tight supervision, simple jobs and clear rewards and sanctions for performance made things easy for bosses and uncomfortable for workers.

In the new world, managers have lost their coercive power. Command and control is over: commitment, persuasion and influence are the new skills that managers must master. Managers have lost their coercive power because:

■ Workers now have choices: if they do not like an employer, there are other employers or social security to fall back on.

- Workers have better education: they can do more, but they expect more. Managers have lost their monopoly on thinking.
- In flat organisations, managers have to make things happen with the help of other departments, and often other firms, over whom they have no direct control. Alliance building and political savvy are new skills to master.
- In a global, virtual world managers increasingly have to manage remote teams: that requires trust, finesse and motivational skill.
- The nature of work has become more ambiguous: you cannot judge productivity by the number of emails sent, or the weight of a report. Managing quality and uncertain workloads requires more judgement and skill than ever.

To succeed in this changing world you have to learn new skills, new ways of working. Intelligence still counts, but being a boffin in a box will not get you to the top. Universities are full of brilliant minds but lousy management. Now you need two new skill sets. First, you have to learn new ways of dealing with people: from command and control to motivating, persuading, coaching, influencing people and dealing with their many different styles. As you look around your own organisation you will find a few people who do this very well, but many more are mediocre at best: it is easy to identify these people skills, much harder to master them.

You need more than intelligence and an ability to handle people well. You also need to manage across the organisation. Managers used to be a cipher between top and bottom of the firm; they would relay orders down and information back up. But no one can last long like that now. Now you have to make things happen with the support of the rest of the organisation. That means making alliances, brokering deals, aligning agendas and building alliances of trust and support. These are intensely political skills. Only the most naive managers think that they can survive without political savvy.

Although the nature of management is becoming more demanding, in theory technology should come to the rescue, at least in part. It should make us more productive and remove much of the dead and inefficient time which was wasted in the past. In practice, technology does not save effort: it raises expectations. We are expected to do more with less; even when we leave the office, the office never leaves us. We wear an electronic ball and chain of email, internet and phone which keeps us constantly shackled to the office. Even if we are physically absent, it is ever harder to find the "off" switch in our minds which lets us relax. We have gone from the life of country club management to 24/7 management, while the workers have gone in the opposite direction.

The need for managers to keep on changing and adapting is mirrored by the need of firms to keep on changing and adapting. The FTSE 100 was set up in 1984. It consisted of the top 100 public companies in the UK. Only 28 survive today. The rest have been overtaken, taken over or gone plain bust. A 72% death rate inside a generation is not good. To survive, it is not enough to manage the status quo. We must always be seeking to change and improve if we are not to join the list of firms that become extinct, and the list of managers who land up on the scrap heap.

Just as firms have to change to stay in the race, so we have to change to stay in the management race. *Management Rules* is a snapshot of best practice as it is today. But it goes further: it looks not just at best practice but also at common practice. A lot of management falls far short of best practice. Most of us have suffered at the hands of a poor manager who thinks that he or she is a great manager. We can learn from bad practice as well as good practice. Bad practice tells us what not to do: if we can avoid the most common mistakes of management, then we will do much better than most of our peers. And bad practice also helps us see why good practice is so good. There is a reason why best practice is good, and bad practice often reveals that reason.

You can read this book any way you want. You can start at the beginning and read through to the end. You can pick and choose which sections to read and which to skip: each section should stand on its own feet. This lets you focus on the areas which are of most interest to you. You can use this book as your personal, just-in-time coach: you can keep it on your desk and refer to it whenever you need advice on a particular subject. And make notes about what works and what does not work for you. Although the principles of best practice may be universal, how you apply those principles will be unique to your style and situation.

This book assumes that you are smart. Each rule and each principle is outlined briefly: you will be smart enough to see how it relates to your daily experience of management, and you can also work out how to put the rule into practice. If you want more detail on any of the principles, you can find plenty of other books to help you. This book gives you the headlines and lets you fill in the detail.

Management Rules sits alongside the *Timeless Lessons of Leadership*. If management is a new art, then leadership is an ancient art. Every year a new theory of leadership emerges, but in practice the essence of good leadership is little changed over the last 5000 years or so. Inevitably, there is some overlap between management and leadership. But I have attempted to keep the overlaps to the minimum, while avoiding too many gaps in either of the books.

Management Rules does not attempt to set out any theory. It simply sets out what works best today. The rules are culled from direct work with over 100 of the best, and a few of the worst, organisations on our planet: they cover every major continent and industry group. This is your handbook to what works today.

MANAGE YOUR TEAM

CHAPTER 1

WHAT YOUR TEAM WANTS FROM YOU

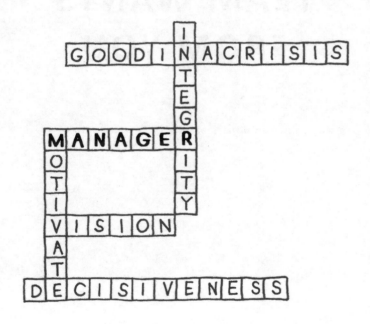

Much has been written about managers and how they can excel. But more or less nothing has been written about what followers expect from their manager. So I spent two years finding out by asking followers across industries and continents what they want from their boss. Followers consistently expect their boss to show five qualities:

- Vision
- Ability to motivate
- Decisiveness
- Good in crises
- Honesty and integrity

From the perspective of your followers, these are the new rules of management. Do well on these qualities, and you will be seen as a good boss.

There is plenty to like about what is in this list, and what is not in this list.

The good news is that the top four qualities can all be learned. And followers do not require their leaders to be charismatic and inspirational. This is just as well: most of us were not born charismatic and you cannot train people to be charismatic. But you must learn how to master the basic skills of management and meet the expectations of your bosses and colleagues. If you do this, you can become devastatingly effective and professional. As a result, people may even start to think you are inspirational.

Words can mean anything, especially on planet business. So the following sections decipher the words that followers use to describe their ideal boss, and show how you can live up to their expectations.

CHAPTER 2

VISION: SETTING A DIRECTION

DO NOT PREDICT
THE FUTURE

Should managers have visions? In the past, managers were mere ciphers between top management and workers: they carried orders down the chain of command and fed information back up. Managers now have to do more: they have to take control and make things happen. So you need a plan, but is that a vision?

Perhaps a vision is too grand. But your team definitely wants to know where they are going and how they are going to get there. You have to give them a sense of direction and purpose. You can do that by telling them a simple story about your direction:

- This is where we are
- This is where we are going
- This is how we will get there

Once you have told them that story, you have given them the vision they want. You are now a fully qualified visionary. As a practical visionary, you do not predict the future; you create the future. That is the purpose of your story.

To make the story really motivational, you add a fourth ingredient: "This is your important role in helping us get there". Show how each team member can contribute and you give them both meaning and purpose. Visions only work when they are personal: each of your team members must see what it means for them. Increasing earnings per share is not a highly motivational vision: creating delighted and loyal customers or achieving a challenging task are more relevant, immediate and motivational visions.

Many things in management which seem sophisticated and complicated are very simple in practice. Visions can be as grand or as simple as you choose.

CHAPTER 3

HOW TO MOTIVATE YOUR TEAM: PRINCIPLES

For the unwary, motivation can be like quicksands. At one end of the spectrum there are the motivational speakers who tell you about climbing up Everest on a pogo stick, naked and backwards. This is meant to inspire us to manage better. At the other end there are the Scrooge-type managers who snarl "Bah! Humbug!" at the mention of motivation or Christmas.

Most of the principles of how to motivate a team are well known. Your team will feel well motivated if they:

■ Work for a worthwhile cause
■ Have a meaningful role
■ Feel supported in their role
■ Have good colleagues
■ Are recognised for their efforts
■ Feel secure as a member of the team

Turn this around for a moment: how motivated would you be if you felt you worked for a worthless firm, had a meaningless role, you got no support, your colleagues sucked, you never got any recognition and you lived in total insecurity?

Within all these basic principles there was one question which consistently predicted whether the boss would be well rated by the team: "My boss takes a personal interest in me and my career" (agree/disagree).

So in all the formal research, humanity peeps through: if we feel well cared for, we respond positively. Find time to invest in each of your team members. Understand who they are and what they want. If you care for them, they will care for you.

If this sounds easy, it isn't. Most managers rated themselves highly on their motivational talent. Most of their followers rated them low. Naturally, most bosses never hear this criticism from their team: either they do not ask or the team is too diplomatic to tell the truth. To put this positively, if you can put in the time and effort to show that you care for your team, you will be well ahead of your peers. You will also find you have a motivated and supportive team.

CHAPTER 4

HOW TO MOTIVATE YOUR TEAM: PRACTICE

MANAGE
BY
WALKING
AWA

You do not need books or psychobabble to work out how to motivate people. Start by thinking about the best boss you have ever worked for. What did the boss do to motivate you so well? Do you do the same things with your team?

In practice, most of us respond to some simple motivational measures. Here are my top ten:

1. Show you care for each member of the team, and for their career. Invest time to understand their hopes, their fears and dreams. Casual time by the coffee machine, not a formal meeting in an office, is the best way to get to know your team members.
2. Say thank you. We all crave recognition: we want to know that we are doing something worthwhile and we are doing it well. Make your praise real, for real achievement. And make it specific. Avoid the synthetic one-minute manager praise ("gee, you typed that email really well . . . ").
3. Never demean a team member. If you have any criticism, keep it private and make it constructive. Don't scold your team members as if they are schoolchildren: treat them as partners and work together to find a way forward.

4. Delegate well. Delegate meaningful work which will stretch and develop your team member. Yes, there is routine rubbish to be delegated, but delegate some of the interesting stuff as well. Be clear and consistent about your expectations.

5. Have a clear vision. Show where your team is going and how each team member can help you all get there. Have a clear vision for each team member: know where they are going and how they can develop their careers.

6. Trust your team. Do not micro manage them. Have courage to implement MBWA: Manage By Walking Away.

7. Be honest. That means having difficult, but constructive, conversations with struggling team members. Don't hide or shade the truth. Honesty builds trust and respect.

8. Set clear expectations. Be very clear about promotion prospects, bonuses and the required outcome of each piece of work. Assume you will be misunderstood: people hear what they want to hear. So make it simple, repeat it often and be consistent.

9. Overcommunicate. Listen twice as much as you speak. Then you will find out what is really

going on, what drives your team members and you can act accordingly.

10. Don't try to be friends. It is more important to be respected than liked: trust endures whereas popularity is fickle and leads to weak compromises. If your team trusts and respects you, they will want to work for you.

As with all things that sound simple, in practice it is very hard to do all of this consistently well. It is high effort, but normally very high reward. A motivated team will climb mountains that unmotivated teams do not even look at.

CHAPTER 5

MAKING DECISIONS IN AN UNCERTAIN WORLD

Being decisive sounds like one of those vague qualities like business sense, or acumen, or charisma which you are either born with or without.

Fortunately, decisiveness is a management art that can be learned. Many management decisions are very easy. It is dealing with the tricky decisions where you prove your worth. Faced with a tricky decision, managers will usually ask themselves a series of questions which will soon decide the answer:

- Do I recognise this pattern? Much of management is pattern recognition. Once you have seen the same movie several times, you know what happens next. Decide accordingly.
- What does my boss want? At worst, this can lead to a game of second guessing which is counter-productive. But you should have a clear idea of the priorities of the boss and of the firm as a whole: this may guide you in one direction or another.
- What does my team want? If the boss is indifferent about which course of action is best, then talk to your team. It is better to run with a decision which they believe in and are committed to

than imposing a decision that may be margin-
ally better but they hate.

■ What are our values? Most firms have basic
beliefs about what is right and wrong: does your
organisation put profits, staff, customers, the
environment or something else first? There is
always a pecking order of values that should
guide you.

Inevitably, these questions may give conflict-
ing guidance. At which point it is worth remembering that decision making is not a rational act
in most organisations. It is a political act which
speaks volumes about perceived priorities. A decision is only as good as the extent to which it is
accepted. The more marginal a decision is, the
more important it is to build a coalition in support
of the decision. You have to spend time working
key decision makers and influencers in private
to come to agreement. The moment you let them
take a public position, they are committed and will
find it hard to change their view without losing
face.

If you have to hold a meeting, never use it to
make a decision. If you give people a decision to

make, they may make the wrong decision. Use the meeting the way the Japanese use meetings: to give public confirmation to the agreements that you have reached in private with each person before you called the meeting. The meeting is about making commitments, not making decisions.

CHAPTER 6

HANDLING CRISES

"This was their finest hour," Churchill thundered when Britain faced its darkest and deepest crisis. And that is how to think of crises: they are the finest hours for any manager. They are the moments when the good are separated from the weak, when you learn and grow the most. They are the times you live life with the record button on; where most of life is lived in drab shades of monochrome, in crises life happens in full and glorious Technicolor. After the crisis is over, you are left with tales to recount.

Don't duck crises, embrace them. They are inevitable in any organisation and any career, so make the most of them.

The principles of crisis management are well known. Here is how not to handle a crisis:

- Deny there is a problem and then act too late. Crises rarely get better of their own accord.
- Go into analysis mode. Analysis is a dangerous substitute for action and is another way of letting the problem grow. Leave analysis until after the event.
- Find someone to blame. This is a great way to make things worse. You will not solve the crisis this way and your attempt to cover your

backside will backfire: once you sling mud, everyone slings mud and everyone gets covered in it. You will not look good.

Here is what you should do:

- Act fast. Don't worry about the things you cannot control: you cannot control them. Focus on what you can do and do it. Even if it is a small thing, it builds momentum and builds confidence.
- Be positive. Followers hate fear, uncertainty and doubt. Be confident and they will happily follow. Do not worry if you take some mis-steps: you can always change direction later. The important thing is to keep up momentum.
- Get help. You cannot do it all yourself, so get help from anyone and everyone who can help you. Do not simply ask your boss for general help: that is called delegating upwards, or giving up. Go to your boss with a plan and be clear about what precisely you need your boss to do to help you. If the boss does not like your plan, then make sure you jointly develop a better one. Make sure you stay in control.

After the event you will be remembered less for what you did and more for how you behaved. If you panic, go missing in action, start pointing the finger of blame, then that is how you will be remembered, even if the crisis was sorted out successfully. But if you appear calm, confident, positive and committed even during the messiest of crises, you will be thought of as someone who is good in a crisis.

Even in a crisis, style counts as much as substance.

CHAPTER 7

HONESTY AND INTEGRITY: DITCH THE ETHICS COURSE

For followers, honesty and integrity has nothing to do with morality and ethics. So you will be spared the tedium of the business school ethics course. Honesty and integrity is much more important than morality: it is all about trust.

Put simply, do you want to work for a boss you do not trust? Occasionally, we have to work for such people, but hopefully not for long.

Perhaps the best way to lose trust is to say "trust me". Never trust anyone who says "trust me". Trust must be built, not claimed. You have three tools for managing trust:

- Values alignment
- Credibility
- Risk

Here they are in more detail.

Values alignment

Understand, respect and possibly share the values of the person you are dealing with. Take time to understand them. Maybe your only point of common interest is a love of gardening, or playing the ukulele. Focus on what you share, not on what divides you. Understand their priorities and perspectives. Inevitably, they will have a different window on reality. And if they come from a different department, they will have different needs and priorities. See how far you can align your interests with theirs. It is far easier to deal with people who are like ourselves: that is one reason diversity remains such a challenge in many organisations.

Credibility

Be reliable. Always deliver on any promise and any expectation. If you can, go beyond expectations. Breaking a promise breaks trust, and once it is broken it is very hard to put back together again. To start with, even small things count: return phone calls promptly, give swift and complete replies to emails. You will only be trusted with big things when you have shown you can be counted on for smaller things. Trust is built incrementally.

Risk

Most people are risk averse. The threat of loss is more powerful than the prospect of a gain. Manage risk. The bigger the risk, the more trust is required. Ask for small commitments before you ask for the big commitment. Find ways of removing risk: show that other people support your way forward; show that doing nothing is even more risky than doing something.

CHAPTER 8

SETTING TARGETS

Management is beset by jargon and acronyms. But, just occasionally, you find an acronym which works. And when it comes to setting targets, there is a popular acronym which helps. Here it is: when you set goals they should be SMART. This is what SMART stands for:

- S – Specific
- M – Measurable
- A – Achievable
- R – Relevant
- T – Time bound

Clearly, this is better than setting vague, unmeasurable, unachievable, irrelevant goals with no deadline. President Kennedy set the nation a goal of "putting a man on the moon within ten years and bringing them back again". It was a classic SMART goal: you may not want to ask your team members to go to the moon, but it is worth understanding why that goal was so effective.

Specific. The goal was highly specific. It was not some vague plea to "get even with the Russians and their Sputnik programme" or to "uphold the technological prowess of our great nation". That is the sort of verbiage politicians like because it sounds good and means nothing. Kennedy was specific and NASA was set up to deliver. And when the goal was achieved NASA lost its way. It had successes (Hubble) and failures (Challenger), but the lack of a specific goal means it has lost focus and drive.

Measurable. The goal was highly measurable and proves that not all goals need to be financial. On planet business there are plenty of measurable nonfinancial goals which are worthwhile: improving customer service and retention, reducing the number of defects, increasing speed to market.

Achievable. This is the dangerous one for managers. The temptation is to set easy goals which can be achieved. That is a recipe for a quiet life of underachievement. Good managers do as President Kennedy did: they ask for the moon. They stretch their team to overperform and they force business not as usual. The result is that the business grows, but so does each team member.

Relevant. Winning the space race against the Soviet Union at the height of the Cold War was clearly a relevant goal. Everyone could see that abandoning space to the undeclared enemy would be a strategic disaster. In the same way, managers need not only to set a goal, they need to explain why it is relevant. They need to show that it is both important and urgent, not just a whim dreamed up on the spur of the moment. When people understand why something is relevant, they will support it and put the effort in.

Time bound. Kennedy did not promise to get to the moon at "some time in the future, maybe". He promised ten years, even although no one knew how, or if, it was possible. The tight time frame gave a sense of focus and urgency which spurred NASA to overcome every setback, including the loss of Gemini astronauts on the launch pad. Now a NASA setback (think Challenger) simply sets NASA back by a year or two. The urgency is gone. Make your goals time bound: only then will you know if the goal has been achieved or not.

CHAPTER 9

HOW TO DELEGATE

THE MORE

S P E C I F I C

YOU ARE NOW, THE LESS LIKELY YOU ARE TO SUFFER UNPLEASANT SURPRISES

Some bosses think that they delegate well when they delegate all the routine rubbish and keep all the interesting work to themselves. These bosses also tend to be very good at delegating the blame when things go wrong.

Clearly, there is an art to delegating well. The principles are simple enough.

■ *Be clear about the objectives.* Don't just ask for a report on the market. That could mean anything of any length. Start by being clear about why you need the report: if it is for the CEO, then that is different from an informal briefing for the team. Then specify the detail. You would not ask a builder to "build a house": you need to be specific about what you want. In the case of a market report you might create a simple story board: outline the sections and headings that you are looking for, and then the team can build around your structure. The more specific you are now, the less likely you are to suffer unpleasant surprises later.

■ *Be clear about timing.* Say what the deadline is and why that deadline exists: is it a brick wall date or is there some flexibility? And this is where you can outline some milestones where you can sit down together and review progress. The more reviews you put in, the less work your team will accomplish: they will spend their time preparing reviews for you rather than doing the work.

■ *Be flexible about the process.* This is the hard bit. When you see a team member doing something differently from how you would do it, there is an overwhelming temptation to intervene. Say nothing, even if that means you have to put sticky tape across your mouth to remain silent. If you intervene, you are no longer delegating and the task has become your task. If you can sit back, then either your team member will succeed in their own way or they will have to correct course, but they will still be responsible for the outcome.

CHAPTER 10

WHAT YOU CAN AND CANNOT DELEGATE

From the manager's perspective, the simple rule is "delegate everything".

There is only one thing you cannot delegate: you cannot delegate your responsibility. As the manager, you are always responsible for the outcomes of your department, whether you delegate all the tasks or none of the tasks. That means you can delegate the praise, but you cannot delegate the blame. If your team messes up, you are responsible for the mess. Bosses several layers up the organisation will have no interest in the "he said she said so I said and they promised but we didn't . . . " discussion. All they know is that you were in charge and you did not deliver.

In terms of tasks, there is very little that a manager cannot delegate. You probably cannot delegate appraisals and pay and performance decisions. You need to decide where you add value and where you want to focus. There are a few things a good manager should do for the team: hire the right people, coach and develop them, get the right budget, manage the higher level politics, make sure everyone has the right jobs and experience. And you may choose to lead one or two initiatives personally. Otherwise, your team should be able to do everything else.

Finally, be brave and delegate your authority. Some managers take great pleasure in controlling everything: you have to ask their permission to make some photocopies. These managers are confused between control and management. Control is about stopping things going wrong and preventing people doing things. Control freaks show they trust no one except themselves. They prefer compliance to commitment. It is a parody of management that is inflicted on much of the long-suffering public sector. Proper management is about enabling people to perform and about gaining the commitment, not just the compliance, of your team.

When you delegate some of your authority, you show trust in your team. Most people respond well to being trusted and are eager to show that they can be trusted more. Delegating authority also gives them the tools to do the job without having to come and ask your permission every hour of the day.

MANAGING OTHER PROFESSIONALS

SET
STRETCHY
GOALS

Some offices are awash with people flaunting one, two or even three degrees. These highly-skilled professionals expect to be managed differently from the masses that sweated their lives out in the factory system.

Professionals typically share some common traits:

■ Good education and high skills, which makes them high value and high cost.
■ High self-esteem: they know they are smart and may well think they are smarter than you. They may quietly resent being managed by someone who they do not necessarily respect, although they will never tell you that.
■ Determination to achieve, and to overachieve. They will see themselves as successful people and will want to prove to themselves that they are successful.

All of this means professionals are high maintenance. The principles for managing them are:

■ *Set stretchy goals.* A bored professional is a dangerous professional. But they want to overachieve, so let them. It is good for the business and good for them: they learn and grow by working to challenging goals.

■ *Undermanage them.* Never micromanage professionals: they will conclude, correctly, that you do not trust them. If they do not feel trusted, they do not feel valued and you have a train crash on your hands.

■ *Give them plenty of recognition.* Feed their self-esteem. They want to know that they are being recognised for doing a meaningful job well.

■ *Be very firm about career, pay and bonus expectations.* Professionals are likely to have high expectations and will latch onto any hint you give them about their prospects. When those prospects do not materialise, watch the toys being thrown out of the pram. Be clear about what expectations they must fulfil if they are to get that bonus or promotion: make them sweat for it.

Ultimately, remember the golden rule: "do unto others as you would have them do unto you". You are a professional: manage others the way you would like to be managed.

CHAPTER 12
HOW TO COACH

Coaching has been given a bad name by some professional coaches who delight in answering every question with a question. This is unfortunate, because coaching is a core skill which every manager needs to learn. Here's why.

Imagine that one of your team comes into your office with a problem. Being a smart manager you know the answer to her problem. You solve her problem. Congratulations, you have just failed as a manager. To see why you failed, let's replay the movie in slow motion and see what really happened.

Your team member came to see you and she had a monkey on her back. You took the screaming monkey off her back. She left happy, and you were left with a screaming monkey. Seeing that you are in a good mood, another team member comes to see you. He also has a screaming monkey on his back. You take that off his back. Over the course of the day, everyone on your team gives you their screaming monkey. By the end of the day, you have a happy team and a room full of screaming monkeys in your office. You are not quite as happy as your team.

In the old world of management, managers were meant to tackle the toughest problems on behalf of their team: that is how they showed they were good managers. But the rules have changed. Managers cannot do it all themselves: they have to help their team perform. That means coaching team members to solve their problems instead of taking the problems away from them.

So how do you coach when you are not a professional coach? Managerial coaching is different from professional coaching. The professional will focus on process; the manager should add some insight and understanding to the coaching process.

Think of coaching as a structured conversation. Each stage of the conversation is like a set of traffic lights: do not proceed until the lights have turned green. The structure can be split into five Os, as follows

■ *Objectives*. What do you want to achieve and what does your team member want to achieve? Clearly, you both want to discover a solution to the problem, which they need to define. You also want to make sure that it is their solution and that they take responsibility for fixing it. If you impose your solution, they will not be committed to it. Be clear about expectations before you start.

■ *Overview*. Ask the team member to explain the situation as clearly as possible. You can add value here by helping the team member see the situation from different perspectives. Ask how the other side see the same situation. You will soon discover that most staff think they are honest, diligent and effective and that their colleagues are devious, incompetent and untrustworthy. What they think of their boss is another matter altogether. As you explore different perspectives you should be developing some ideas about what the solution might be. Careful questioning will nudge your team member in the direction of finding the right solution.

■ *Options*. Once you are satisfied that you have a good overview of the situation, you can ask your team member for possible solutions. Do not fix immediately on one take-it-or- leave-it option. Encourage some creativity. This will improve the quality of the solution, and by creating choice it gives your team member more ownership over the option which they pick. And make sure it is their choice, not yours. An imposed solution is not a solution they will own or feel committed to. There is a risk they may even come up with a better solution than the one you had in mind.

■ *Obstacles*. With a good option agreed, it is tempting to think that the job is done. Tempting, but wrong. Ask your team member to identify potential pitfalls and obstacles to the solution, and then work out how to deal with them. You want to avoid the situation where your team member rushes off enthusiastically and then falls at the first hurdle which they had not anticipated.

■ *Outcomes*. Finally make sure that you have agreed what you think you have agreed. It is human nature to hear what we want to hear. You may think they are going to do all the work; they may be waiting for you to do something for them first. So ask your team member to summarise what they think happens next: see if their version of reality is the same as yours.

As with any technique, at first coaching seems awkward and unnatural. Over time it becomes second nature. And in the short term it is always easier to solve the problem yourself. But in the longer term, coaching is an investment which pays good dividends: you will help your team be more self-sufficient, they will take more problems away from you. And they may even think you are a good boss, because you help them develop and grow.

MANAGE THE ORGANISATION

TAKE CONTROL

JUST BECAUSE YOU HAVE BEEN MADE A MANAGER, IT DOES NOT MEAN YOU ARE IN CONTROL

The best book you never need to read is called *Control your Destiny or Someone Else Will*, written by legendary General Electric CEO Jack Welch. The reason you do not need to read it is that the title is the message: take control or someone else will.

Just because you have been made a manager, it does not mean you are in control. Never confuse position and power. Even Prime Ministers are not always in control: John Major was often accused of being in office, but not in power.

When you are appointed to a new post, you have to take control fast. Here is how.

1. *Have a plan.* Set out your vision, which shows where you intend to go and how you intend to get there. If you have no plan, you have no direction. The best plans are the simplest: if the CEO drops by, you should be able to explain in ten seconds or less what your group does and what your goals are. A plan is often a simple story around a theme such as:
   - We will cut costs
   - We will raise quality
   - We will be more customer focused

- We will go to market faster than the competition
- We will professionalise our way of working

From that simple theme, you can drive a plan which involves setting targets, training, new measures and evaluations and perhaps a new team structure.

2. *Set expectations.* Never simply accept the plan left to you by your predecessor: he or she will have promised that sales will triple, costs fall and profits will go through the roof thanks to their brilliant stewardship of the department. If you accept this, you are dead meat. Any success will be down to the brilliant plan of your predecessor. If you fall short, you will have failed. When you start, find all the skeletons in all the cupboards and put them on display. Show that it will take a manager of rare genius, humanity and determination to avoid total collapse in your department. Set expectations low. And then your modest performance can be seen as a big success.

3. *Find the right team.* Do not assume that the team you inherit is the team you have to live with. The team will be a mix of the good, the

bad, and the essential but coasting experts. Having a B (or second choice) team is a recipe for sleepless nights. And you will find one or two team members occupy most of your time: they are the source of most problems and are often high maintenance personally. Move them out of your team: either sell them to another part of the organisation or talk to HR about moving them out altogether. This sends a strong signal that you are now in control. And by having a team you know and trust, you will be able to deliver your plan.

4. *Get the right support.* Perhaps the most important thing a manager can do for the team is to make sure the team has enough budget and that they have enough political support to fulfil their duties. Doing this alone can be nearly a full-time task. But if you do not control the politics, they will control you.

CHAPTER 14

BUILD YOUR TRUSTED NETWORK

All managers need a network of influence that spreads beyond their formal area of control. Management used to be about making things happen through people you controlled: now it is about making things happen through people you do *not* control at all or partially control, as well as through people you do control. Management has become harder.

At the heart of influence is trust: we will work with people we trust much more readily than people we do not trust. We will do favours for people we trust in the knowledge that such favours are likely to be reciprocated in the future. Trust is the oil in the machine which makes both firms and managers work well: without trust, the machinery of the firm grinds to a halt.

You can think of trust as a simple formula:

$$T = (V \times C) / R$$

To put this into English:

Trust (T) increases in proportion to Values Alignment (V) and Credibility (C), but decreases in proportion to the perceived Risk (R) of the situation.

Here is how you can put this equation to use to build your trust and influence in your firm:

Values alignment. For better or worse, we find it easier to trust people who are like ourselves. We value intimacy, even as we declare unwavering belief in diversity. So find some common ground when building trust: common friends, colleagues, experiences, past times, educational background. And the best way to do this is to let people talk about their favourite subject: themselves. The more they talk and the more you listen, the more common ground you can find. Avoid the natural instinct to compete by showing that you have an even better holiday, experience, car or whatever.

Credibility. Without credibility, there can be no trust. Remember the inscription above the monumental James A. Farley post office in New York: "neither snow nor rain nor heat nor gloom of night stays these couriers from the swift completion of their appointed rounds". Like the New York postman, you must always deliver. And that means managing expectations. If you are not sure that you can deliver, say so. Even if you half commit with plenty of caveats, what you say will not be what is remembered: your commitment will be remembered and your caveats will be forgotten because people hear what they want to hear.

Credibility starts with small things: following up on a meeting swiftly, sending through some promised notes immediately. Your credibility grows slowly, one act at a time. Although credibility is slow to build it is fast to lose. Trust is also slow to build and fast to lose. When you fail to deliver you find that trust is like a porcelain vase: it is very hard to put back together again once it is broken. The only remedy is to avoid losing credibility in the first place.

CHAPTER 15

INFLUENCING DECISIONS

Decision making in firms can be very opaque. Only the most naive manager believes that decisions follow formal decision-making processes. If you submit your report and hope for the best, then prepare for the worst: you will be disappointed. To make sure you get the decision you want, you have to hustle. Fortunately, "hustle" was defined by Daniel Kahnemann, who won the Nobel Prize for his work on decision-making heuristics (short cuts, to you and me). Here are seven principles of decision making and how you can put them to your advantage:

1. *Anchoring.* The motto of the Welsh Rugby team in the 1980s was "get your retaliation in first", which is what anchoring is all about. Don't wait for the planning group to announce that each department is expected to achieve 10% budget reduction next year. Set your stall out early that your department expects to achieve great things next year with a paltry 20% increase in budget. Would you rather have your budget discussion anchored around a 10% decrease or a 20% increase in budget?

2. *Repetition.* Repetition works, repetition works, repetition works, repetition works, repetition

works, repetition works, repetition works. What does repetition do? It works. All great dictators and all great advertisers know this: repeat something often enough and people start to believe that Stalinism is great or that an expensive cream can take 20 years off your face.

3. *Social proof.* If Wayne Rooney and Tiger Woods use the gear, then perhaps if we buy the same gear we might play as well as they do. Some hope, but endorsements are powerful. Find a powerful sponsor in your firm who is prepared to endorse your position, and suddenly you will find people are more prepared to take you seriously.

4. *Emotional intensity.* Read the newspapers and you will see that they use this trick all the time. They can report that crime statistics are up, down or sideways and our eyes glaze over. And then they have a picture of a granny who was mugged and her heartrending story, and suddenly the story becomes compelling. Do not rely just on statistics: use theatre to bring them to life. If customer service levels are dipping, get a video of an irate customer: much harder for anyone to deny. Note that CEOs spend a lot of time walking the halls and talking to people,

precisely because they want to get to the truth behind all the numbers and reports that land on their desk.

5. *Restricted choice.* If you are offered a choice between 25 sorts of mobile phone on 30 different types of tariff, you will reasonably feel overwhelmed. Equally reasonably, you will feel that, whatever choice you make, you may well have left a better choice on the table. You will suffer regret if you choose from such a wide choice. Many people take the easy route out: they make no choice at all. But a crafty salesperson will give you a choice of just three options: you can clearly see which is best. You make the choice and feel good about it. Do not overwhelm managers with choices: give them two or three clear options; and make sure the option you prefer is the one which they are bound to choose.

6. *Loss aversion.* Let's toss a coin. If you choose right, you win £11,000. If you choose wrong, you lose £9000. Logically, you should feel good about this: on balance you will come out ahead, especially if you are allowed many tosses of the coin. But not many people would go for this deal: the risk of the loss is far worse than the potential gain. We are loss averse. For manag-

ers, this also means risk aversion. So remove the perceived risk from your proposals, and increase the perceived risk of doing nothing. Put loss aversion to work for you.

7. *Framing.* Do you prefer savings and investment or cuts and spending? Easy choice, except that they are the same thing. Frame the discussion to suit your needs. Language counts. An investment or medical operation with a 90% success rate sounds good. How do you feel about a 10% chance of going bust or dying? The same information presented in different ways leads to different decisions. Frame information the way it will get the decision you want.

CHAPTER 16

NEGOTIATING YOUR BUDGET

NEGOTIATE
YOUR
BUDGET
HARD

Each budget cycle brings a choice:

■ Accept the mandated budget and then work like crazy to deliver against a very challenging target; you will struggle for any bonus.

■ Negotiate like crazy for one month to get a sensible budget and then have eleven months delivering the budget relatively easily and getting a good bonus.

If you are sensible, you negotiate your budget hard. Here is how.

Anchor the debate early. The planning department may think 10% cost reduction is a good idea. Before they even pronounce, you need to sow the idea that your group is in growth mode and that 20% growth is the very minimum needed to deliver what is required. Anchor the debate around 20% growth, not 10% cuts.

Use your data. You know what is happening in your area better than anyone else. Paint a picture of rampant competition, rapacious customers and suppliers and a world in which it will be a miracle of heroic management simply to maintain last year's performance. Keep hammering

away: eventually, the planners will go away and
search for easier prey.

Cut a deal with top management. Understand what
top management really want and expect; align
what you are doing with what they want. You will
find the strategic imperatives of the firm can
trump the number-crunchers who plan the
budgets.

Manage this year's performance, and how it is perceived. Of course, you should want to overachieve. But if you have a stellar year, management
will assume that is the baseline performance for
next year. So bring costs forward, delay revenue
recognition if you are overperforming. And make
it clear that this year is driven by unrepeatable
one-off factors.

CHAPTER 17

MANAGING YOUR BUDGET

Managing budgets is one of the basic disciplines which all managers must master. There is both a logical and political reality to managing budgets. That means managers have to master both the discipline and the game-playing of budget management.

First, it helps to understand the annual budget cycle. It always ends in a crisis. Most of the time, the crisis is about closing a performance gap. The gap may be in another part of the firm, but you will still be expected to help close the gap. The gap comes about because departments overspend, costs go up, sales flag. It does not matter why the crisis came about: you will be expected to help out.

By the time the crisis comes, it will be too late to close the gap by increasing sales. The only realistic option is that you will have to cut your budget. So your annual budget planning should take account of the inevitable year end squeeze.

Best practice says you should manage your budget on a 48/52 basis: spend 48% of your budget and achieve 52% of your goals in the first six months. This leaves some contingency for the last six months. In theory you then break down the first two quarters on a further 48/52 basis. Best practice allows you to be squeezed heavily in the last quarter. This matters because:

■ To achieve a 48/52 split, you probably have to put all your discretionary spend into the last quarter. So you lose your discretionary spend, which is likely to be the spending closest to your heart.

■ You simply set yourself a higher hurdle for the following year: next year's budget will be based on your ability to overperform against this year's budget.

In practice, you probably want to aim for something like a 51/53 budget split. Spend 51% of your budget and achieve 53% of your goals in the first half, and then split the first two quarters of the year the same way. That means you spend fast and achieve fast in the first quarter. Here is how you do it:

■ Spend fast means you spend your discretionary budget early. If you want to invest in training, a conference, some research, a test market, then do it in the first quarter. This is exactly the sort of spend which will be squeezed in the last quarter. Spend while you can.

■ If you have managed the previous year well, you will have hidden some prospective sales at the end of the previous year. Then as soon as the new year starts, you announce the new sales and your performance is turbo boosted from the start.

As the year unfolds, take advantage of any staffing changes. If you have budget to hire more people, delay the hires for a couple of months. If staff leave, do not replace them for a couple of months. This timing effect adds up to a healthy pot of cost savings which you can keep in reserve for when a rainy day comes.

CONTROLLING BUDGETS

THE BUDGET IS A CONTRACT BETWEEN TWO MANAGERS

At some point you will be the poacher who turns gamekeeper. As a junior manager, you play the normal budget games. As a senior manager, you have to delegate budget responsibility to other managers who will now be playing those games against you. The good news is that you will recognise most of the games. The bad news is that when they are played well, they are very hard to defend against.

When you control delegated budgets, there are some basic principles to remember:

Stay on top of the budget. Never accept excuses for why a budget report should be delayed: that is always a sign that something is wrong.

Watch the phasing of the budget. Aim for a 48/52 split: not more than 48% of the costs and at least 52% of the results in the first half of the year. Clearly, adjust this for the expected overall growth or decline of the business over the year.

Look beyond the formal budget numbers. You should know your area well enough to recognise whether exceptional costs or revenues are going to emerge. You also need to look for sandbagging: is the team hoarding cost savings or revenues for a rainy day. Only when you look beyond the formal numbers can you have any confidence in the forecast for the rest of the year.

Look for LEO. LEO is the "Latest Expected Outcome" for the year. This is your early warning system: make sure your team forecasts accurately so that you can take corrective action as early as possible. The longer the year progresses, the harder it is to make adjustments.

The budget is the budget is the budget. The budget is a contract between managers: "I promise to deliver the following results for the following budget". Hold your team to the contract they agreed. They will try to change the rules by measuring themselves against reforecast budgets, revised budgets and more. Don't let them off the hook.

You own all cost savings. Praise your team for making cost savings, but do not let them spend all the cost savings automatically. Let them have some of the savings, so that they are encouraged to make more. But you need to balance the savings which one team makes with the inevitable losses and setbacks in other areas.

Cash and accruals are different. Focus on accruals. Cash only recognises what has come in and gone out of the door. Accruals recognises commitments that have been made but the cash has not yet been spent. Accruals gives you a better idea of where your budget is heading. Not all of your team will recognise the difference.

Make friends with the financial controller and book keeper. They are your eyes and ears, and good ones will alert you early to any problems.

CHAPTER 19

HANDLING BAD NEWS

Cock-ups happen, even in the most illustrious career. How you handle cock-ups determines whether your career will be short-lived, or whether it can continue on its glorious path. It pays to know how to handle cock-ups before they happen: in the heat of the moment, it is far too easy to do the wrong thing and to make matters worse.

Here is how to handle the inevitable setbacks which will happen to you:

- *Accept responsibility.* Do not waste time trying to shift the blame. Your boss will have no interest in the "I said she said but I meant and anyway he didn't and they promised" debate. The more mud you throw, the more mud will land on you. Best clear the mud up, rather than throw it around.
- *Offer a solution.* Never delegate a problem upwards. It is better to offer an imperfect solution than no solution. When you offer a solution you move from a negative analysis of what went wrong on to a positive discussion about what happens next.
- *Act fast.* Bad news does not magically become good news all by itself. Mostly bad news tends to get worse as events spiral out of control.

You need to stay in control of events. Once you lose control of events you lose control of your fate. Do not rely on the generosity of others when things go wrong.

- *Communicate early.* The worst thing to happen is for your boss to hear the bad news from his or her boss. If this happens, you have made your boss look like an idiot who does not even know what is going on in his or her area of control. You will not be thanked for letting this happen.
- *Stay positive.* Style counts as much as substance. If you sound and act negative, you invite others to act the same way. If you are consistently positive and action focused it is much harder for others to act negatively, and you will leave a good impression behind long after the details of the bad news saga have been forgotten.

Doing all of this takes some courage and requires personal resilience. The natural instinct is to hide, prevaricate, shift the blame and hope that somehow the bad news evaporates. These are natural, but fatal, instincts.

Most bosses recognise that cock-ups happen and can be remarkably forgiving about them: they have been there, too. And the more experience you get of handling cock-ups, the better you get at dealing with them. First time around, the instinct is to panic. Eventually, you will scarcely break into a sweat and the five principles above will be as natural as breathing air.

CHAPTER 20

PROJECT MANAGEMENT

SIMPLICITY
TRIUMPHS OVER
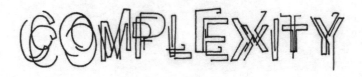

Project management is a core skill which all managers must master. Fortunately, you do not need to master the 40 separate activities and seven different processes of a qualified PRINCE2 practitioner to be able to manage a project. With project management, as with much of management, simplicity triumphs over complexity.

The seven basic principles of project management are:

1. *Start at the end.* Forget the trite nonsense about "first things first". The first thing to do is to be very clear about the end goal: if you do not know where you are going, you are unlikely to get there. Make sure your goal is a SMART goal. Avoid scope creep, where more and more objectives get added to the project. One clear goal is better than two. By the time you have three objectives, you have a recipe for confusion.

2. *Work back from the end.* Identify the minimum number of steps required to complete the project. Ignore the detail for the moment: you can always make things more complicated later.

3. *Identify the key milestones* you must hit to get to the goal. Your minimum number of steps should fall into a logical order: design the house,

put in the foundations and do the decoration only at the end. Each step should have a finish date: you have now identified the major phases and timing of your project.

4. *Identify any long lead time items* which need to be worked on now. Even something in Steps 5 or 7 may need to be prepared now. One conversation today with a top executive might save weeks later on.

5. *Develop a more detailed work plan* for your first step. Break this step into bite-sized chunks which can be accomplished quickly. This ensures you build momentum and enables you to track progress. If a step is too large it can be discouraging: reduce into small and simple steps, and it becomes do-able.

6. *Identify any obstacles or threats* that might derail your project. Work out how to avoid them (best) or to deal with them if they arise.

7. *Make sure you have the right support* to deliver your project. Do not even start until you have this. Support includes both budget and people. The people may include team members who work full time on your project. Hold out for the best people: if you get the B team, you commit yourself to stress and to sleepless nights. Finding

the right people also means ensuring you have the right political backing from bosses and peers so that the project can happen.

When projects fail, they fail in their own unique and messy way. Here are some of the most common pitfalls of project management and how you can mess up:

- Be unclear about the goals.
- Change your specifications frequently.
- Be slow in making decisions, so you hold up the entire programme. Then change your mind frequently.
- Fall in love with the process: draw up risk logs, issue logs, activity logs, meeting logs, phone logs, master logs and more. You will log every-thing and do nothing.
- Assume it will all work out. Projects always go wrong: people don't deliver, obstacles appear. To minimise these problems, follow up on promises and commitments; put in place effec-tive governance and simple project tracking so that you can see when things are not happening and take corrective action fast.
- Get the wrong team on board.

MANAGE YOUR COLLEAGUES

CHAPTER 21

MANAGING YOUR PEERS

Your **real** competition is sitting at a desk near you.

Who is your greatest competitive threat? The conventional answer is to look in the marketplace and see your nearest rival. But for most managers, your real competition is sitting at a desk near you. Your marketplace rivals can steal your market share. Your peers compete for things which are far more important to you today: they compete for a limited budget pot, potential promotions and bonuses and for management time and support.

Although your colleagues are your greatest competitors, they are also vital to helping you make things happen. So you have a schizophrenic relationship with your peers. You compete and collaborate at the same time. This is not always how it was. In times gone by, managers sat in comfortable functional silos and any coordination across silos happened at the top of the firm. Now managers live in the matrix. The standard operating procedure is for you to have responsibilities that far exceed your formal authority. To bridge the gap between your authority and responsibility you need to build a network of trust and influence across the organisation. With this web of support you can make things happen. Without the web you will struggle.

This new world adds a new dimension to the skills a manager must master. In the old world, managers had to have high IQ (be smart). Then we discovered that management was about people so managers had to have high EQ (emotional quotient). But look around your firm and you can find plenty of people who have high IQ and EQ who languish in the backwaters. Meanwhile, people who are not so smart and not so nice mysteriously rise to the top. Something is missing. That something is PQ: political quotient.

PQ is the art of making things happen through people you do not control. So management is not just about old world control. The new rules of management demand that managers learn the subtle arts of persuasion and influence. Persuasion means getting someone to do something once, which is relatively easy. Influence is a higher order skill: it is about building a willing alliance of people who will help you time and time again. For that, you need trust and credibility and not just formal authority.

This section looks at how you can acquire the subtle arts of influence, build your network of trust and support and raise your PQ: political quotient.

CHAPTER 22

STYLES OF MANAGEMENT: THE THEORY

OTHER PEOPLE ARE NOT LIKE YOU

Management is about making things happen through other people. The challenging piece of that equation is "other people", because other people are not like you – which may or may not be a good thing. And you cannot understand your own style until you understand how it affects other people. There is no right or wrong: there is only what works and what does not.

"Other people" not only have different priorities and perspectives, they also have different ways of thinking and different ways of working. Our first experience of this is when we acquire our first boss and find we have to adapt to their odd ways of working if we are to make any progress. And the same holds true when you deal with your peers: you have to find a way of adapting to their style of working, if you are to make any progress.

There is an entire industry devoted to understanding the different ways people work. Perhaps the grandparent of all approaches to management styles, and the one which is most commonly used, is the Myers Brigg Type Indicators (MB/TI). It takes years to master this system, which rather defeats its purpose: the idea is not to master MB/TI but to be able to manage through people not like yourself.

Nevertheless, it is a good start: it highlights some of the ways in which people differ from each other. Take a look at the chart below. As you look at the positive impact of each characteristic, you will be forgiven for thinking that you have all the positive qualities of a manager. That is not how MB/TI works. You have to choose between E and I, S and N, T and F, and J and P. You then come up with an acronym such as ENTP or ISTJ to judge your style. MB/TI has a box for everyone, although you should not be put in a box until you are dead.

If you have trouble deciding which style you are, look at the negative impact of each style. Normally, that makes it very easy to see which style you are not. The original MBTI insists that all styles are equal and that there is no "wrong" style. The reality is that there is a dark side to every style, and you probably want to think about the dark side of your style. It might not matter to you because you have learned to live with it: it may matter hugely to your peers or, worse, your boss.

MB/TI highlights the importance of having a mix of styles on your team. If everyone is an extrovert, then you will have the chaos of a chimpanzee's tea party on your hands. If everyone is an introvert, then your team will echo to the sound of silence. Balance is good.

Type	Description	Positive impact	Negative impact
Extroversion (E)	Gains energy from others Speaks, then thinks	Spreads energy, enthusiasm	Loud mouth, does not include other people
Introversion (I)	Gains energy from within, thinks before speaks	Thoughtful, gives space to others	Nothing worth saying? Uneasy networker
Sensing (S)	Observes outside world More facts, less ideas	Practical, concrete, detailed	Dull, unimaginative
Intuitive (N)	Pays attention to self, inner world, idea	Creative, imaginative	Flighty, impractical, unrealistic
Thinking (T)	Decides with the head and logic	Logical, rational, intellectual	Cold and heartless

(Continued)

Type	Description	Positive impact	Negative impact
Feeling (F)	Listens to the heart	Empathetic, understanding	Soft headed, fuzzy thinker, bleeding heart
Judging (J)	Organised, scheduled, tidy	High work ethic, focused and reliable	Compulsive neat freak Uptight, rigid, rule bound
Perceiving (P)	Keeps options open, opportunistic	Work–life balance, enjoys work	Lazy, messy, aimless and unreliable

CHAPTER 23

MANAGING DIFFERENT STYLES: THE PRACTICE

GOOD MANAGERS ARE LIKE CHAMELEONS AND WILL ADAPT TO EACH SITUATION

You do not need to be a genius to realise that different people have different styles. As long as you can still fog a mirror, you will know this to be true. Different sorts of psychologists and consulting firms all have their unique ways of categorising people and they all have their own best theory on what you are meant to do about it. For a not so small fee, they will tell you. You can find an outline of many approaches on the web.

For free, you can observe your colleagues and come up with your own jargon-free list of different ways of working. Here are a few of the common ways in which managers work, arranged as a series of trade-offs. You can add more trade-offs yourself.

As an exercise think of your boss, or someone else you need to influence. As you look at the list, circle the four characteristics that best define the most important biases in the way your boss works. For instance, some people work like crazy during the week and it is very hard to get their attention: on Friday afternoons they wind down and chill out. That is the perfect time to talk to them and have a constructive conversation. You will not find that in any psychological profiling system, but it is the sort of commonsense you have to use to influence your colleagues.

Big picture vs. Detail

Judging vs. Sensing

Positive vs. Cynical

Task focus vs. People focus

Open vs. Defensive

Controlling vs. Empowering

Analysing vs. Action

Outcomes vs. Process

Inductive vs. Deductive

Prompt vs. Tardy

Quick vs. Slow

Rash vs.Contemplative

Morning vs. Afternoon

Written vs. Spoken word

Numbers vs. Words

Email vs. Face to face

Once you have identified the major biases in the way your boss works, you have also identified what you need to do to work with your boss. If you share the same biases, you are lucky. More likely, you will find that you have to adapt your style. Good managers know how to do this instinctively: they are like chameleons and will adapt to each situation. Weak managers plough on with their own style and when they get no response they simply shout louder, work harder and wonder why they get no response.

When colleagues clash, it is often because of style differences. Your task is to find the tune that each person dances to, then play that tune. When you succeed, the effect is obvious even if no one can quite work out how you manage to get along with so many people so well. You can choose to share your secret or not, as you will.

CHAPTER 24

PUTTING PRAISE AND FLATTERY TO WORK

Recent research confirms what we all suspected: flattery works. But the research goes further: there is no point at which flattery becomes counterproductive. In other words, the more you flatter, the better.

The research makes sense in the real world. Most people who work in an organisation feel under-recognised, under-rewarded and under-promoted. We can never quite accept that the oddball we knew from years ago got the promotion which we clearly deserved. If we feel we live in a cruel, uncaring and unfair world, then we are not alone in our feelings.

And then into this cruel and uncaring world steps someone who recognises our innate honesty, humanity, diligence and downright genius. Not surprisingly, we find it easy to respect that person's very fine judgement.

This is wonderful news for managers. Most managers do not offer much in the way of praise. It does not feel very business-like: managers prefer to prove themselves by dealing with challenges rather than celebrating successes. So if you are the one manager who takes time to recognise and praise achievement, you will stand out. And you will find you grow a network of people who like you and respect you for the way you treat them.

And if you take time to praise your team, that is even better. Praise from a boss is music to most people's ears.

Giving praise is not that painful, once you get used to it. Nor does it take much time or effort. So it is a cheap and easy way of building your reputation and building a committed and enthusiastic team.

There are good ways and bad ways of giving praise. Here is how not to do it:

- Avoid condescending to someone: "Gee, I am so happy you managed to polish your shoes today. . . .".
- Avoid the trite one-minute-manager synthetic praise: "Wow, you photocopied that page so well!"
- Avoid generic praise: "You are a totally awesome human being!" means nothing unless there is a specific context and reason for saying so.
- Avoid always praising the same people; they will become your pets and everyone else will resent the special treatment you give them.

■ Avoid name checking. CEOs and Hollywood actresses go in for name checking everyone and their parrots for their success. By the time they have got to the fiftieth name the audience have become zombies and the praise has lost any semblance of credibility.

Here is how you can praise well:

■ Praise in public. Praise is about recognition: private recognition is good, but public recognition is even better.
■ Make your praise specific. Be clear about what someone did and why it made a difference.
■ Make your praise personal. Find something unique about the individual you are praising, and show how they have helped you and the difference it has made to you.

Be generous in your praise. Managers often make the mistake of thinking that if they give praise, then they surrender credit for a success. The opposite is true. The more you give praise for a success, the more you become associated with the success. Giving praise is a subtle way of claiming the credit for successes.

CHAPTER 25

PERSUASIVE CONVERSATIONS

MOST
PEOPLE ARE
NOT
PSYCHIC

It is fashionable to talk about having "difficult conversations" with your peers. Who wants a difficult conversation when you can have a productive conversation? The key to having a productive conversation is to follow a logical structure. The structure allows you as much creativity and flexibility as you want in what you say: it is not a script. And it takes from a few moments to a few years: it is quicker to persuade someone to have lunch with you than it is to persuade your firm to start a bank or a new business.

Social conversations can meander on. That is part of their pleasure. A persuasive conversation cannot meander: it has to be structured to achieve your goal. Think of the structure as a series of traffic lights which are all at red. You cannot proceed to the next part of the conversation until the traffic light in front of you has turned green. Cross a red light and you might get lucky, but you might have a car crash. Your choice.

As you look at the structure, remember the Noddy principle. The idea is to get the other person nodding with you: get them into the habit of agreeing with you. At the start they may simply agree with you that there is a lot of weather today. Then keep them gently nodding until you reach the final agreement.

Remember PASSION and you can remember the structure. Here is what PASSION stands for.

P: Preparation

Know what you want from the conversation and what the next steps are. You might want agreement to your idea; you might want to progress your idea just one step. Perhaps you want to get some information, or get a referral to another executive. And have a plan B. If you cannot get your ideal outcome, have a back up.

Preparation also means putting yourself in the shoes of the other person: what are they likely to be thinking? How will they see the same issue? Why might they object? Where is the common ground you can build on?

Finally, preparation means being crystal clear about the logistics: who, what, where and when. If it is a big meeting, do not rush to the meeting at the last moment. Arrive in plenty of time so that you can be relaxed and 100% focused on the meeting, not on whether you will arrive in time.

A: Alignment

Take time to get on the same wavelength as the other person. If you do not know them well, take time to establish some personal trust: identify some common interests, common background, people you know in common. If you know them well, check that you are seeing them at a good time, not when they are beating their heads against the wall.

If you are developing a new relationship, perhaps all you want to do in the entire meeting is establish some rapport over lunch. You can then leave the rest of the conversation to another time.

S: Situation review

If you don't know the question, you can't know the answer. The situation review is about making sure that you are both answering the same question. You may have a very important idea or issue, but it might be irrelevant to the other person. You have to see the world through their eyes if you are to stand a chance of persuading them. So let them talk. The more they talk, the more you find out about how they are thinking, and the easier it is for you to align your interests with theirs.

S: So what's in it for me?

Once you have fully understood the situation from their perspective, summarise. And in the summary suggest a desired outcome that you can both agree on. The outcome is a benefit which answers the simple question "what's in it for me?".

I: Idea, stated simply

Once you have agreed on the desired outcome you can state your idea about how to get there. You should know enough about the situation from the other person's perspective to be able to pitch the idea in language they like.

O: Overcome objections

The best way to overcome objections is to pre-empt them. If you have understood the situation properly, you will be able to pitch your idea in a way that pre-empts any concerns there may be. Alternatively, overcome objections by agreeing with them. Agree with an objection? Agree that the person has raised a valid point, one that other people have had or you have been worried about. And then talk through how other people have resolved the issue.

The worst way of dealing with an objection is to fight it: you then set up a win–lose discussion in which you may win on logic, but you lose a friend.

N: Next steps

Most people are not psychic. They will not know what you and they are meant to do next. You have to spell it out and then ask them for confirmation. Do not assume that they have listened and agreed.

Finally, make sure you follow up. Again, do not assume that the next steps will happen all by themselves. You will need to push. And it always helps to send a quick thank-you note for the meeting, with a reminder about what next steps are due by when.

CHAPTER 26

HOW TO SAY "NO"

BEING NEGATIVE IS A CARDINAL SIN

At some point you need to find a way of saying no to the latest insane idea to have come out of the head of your boss or one of your peers. And in the corporate world, being negative is a cardinal sin, so you have to be positive about "no". How do you square this circle? You have several options:

- *Do nothing.* The hardest thing in the world to overcome is corporate inertia. The simple act of doing nothing puts all the pressure on the person with the idea to create some momentum. Most of the time they will either give up, or someone else will quietly get a gun out and put the idea out of its misery. Your hands will be clean.
- *The judo throw.* Agree that the idea is addressing a really important issue and that you are ready to help. Of course, you need to find a way of getting it past all the evil monsters in other departments, so you will find a way of presenting it to them so it is acceptable to them. By the time you have agreed these "presentational" issues you will have redesigned the whole idea to your liking. This is often the most constructive and powerful way of saying "no".

■ *Pass the buck.* This comes in two flavours. Agree that the idea is great from your perspective, but of course you are the wrong person to deal with it: volunteer someone else. Alternatively, agree that the idea is great and suggest that there are other departments which need to endorse the idea. Take the idea to the other departments and present it in such a way that they will kill it for you.

■ *The nice save.* Find just one aspect of the idea, however small, which you can enthusiastically endorse. Be enthusiastic about it, and then find a way of building up that part of the idea, while quietly downplaying the rest of the idea. By the time you finish you will, as with the judo throw, have redesigned the idea to your taste.

With each of these approaches you never have to say no, you are not negative and you are not obstructive: you are a good team player. At worst you are passive (because, of course, you are overwhelmed with other work), or you are positively supportive. But just occasionally the best thing you can do is to go into a quiet room with your colleague and just say no. If you have good reasons for your position and you can suggest some positive alternatives, then your honesty may well be appreciated. But make sure you avoid a public battle which will harm you both.

CHAPTER 27

HOW TO DEAL WITH MR AND MRS NASTY

LOOK
THE
PART,
DON'T
LOOK
THE
FOOL

Mr and Mrs Nasty can be your boss, your customers or your colleagues. You may not want to deal with them, but you have to deal with them. The question is how, especially when tempers and the temperature start to rise and it is hard to stay cool.

There are two sure fire ways of making things worse:

1. Argue the righteous logic of your position. Fighting emotion with logic is like fighting fire with petrol: spectacular, but not advisable.
2. Get emotional. As soon as you descend into the sewer with Mr Nasty, he will get on his high horse and trumpet how unreasonable you are. He wins, you lose.

So if neither logic nor emotion works, what does?

The goal is simple to state, hard to achieve. You need to do the following:

- *Stay positive and professional.* How you behave is as important as what you say. Look the part, don't look the fool.
- *Focus on the desired outcome.* Where do you want to be at the end of the conversation? Work

towards that end and avoid getting dragged into the mire. As a rule, it is better to win a friend than to win an argument.

■ *Focus on common interests, not on narrow positions.* At its simplest, a position may be: "You messed up". The common interest is "we need to find a solution".

So how do you stay positive when Mr and Mrs Nasty are doing their best to enrage you? I have asked many executives this question, and here are some of the best answers I have heard:

■ *Imagine what your favourite role model would do in this situation,* and then do the same thing. If your role model is a mix of Darth Vader and Vlad the Impaler, do not use this technique.

■ *Become a fly on the wall and watch the event.* As you detach you will be able to think more clearly and objectively, without getting emotionally involved.

■ *Imagine Mr Nasty in a pink tutu.* It is hard to get angry with a fat 50-year-old in a pink tutu. Not laughing (or being sick) may be a greater challenge than staying calm.

■ *Pull out your imaginary Uzi and splatter their brains over the wall.* As Mr Nasty does not even know what you have done, he cannot retaliate.

■ *Count to ten, just like your gran told you to.* Let the immediate flush of anger pass and regain control of your feelings.

■ *Breathe deeply, as taught in Buddhist meditation lessons.* Like counting to ten, this allows you to regain control and lets you respond professionally.

Finally, remember that happiness is the greatest revenge. Mr and Mrs Nasty are nasty today and probably have nasty lives. That is their problem. They may make you stressed today, but tomorrow you will be happy and they will not. You have won.

CHAPTER 28

PROFESSIONAL GUARD

MOST TRAPS ARE OBVIOUS AND AVOIDABLE

There is nothing the newspapers like more than a good scandal, preferably involving drugs, royalty and deviant sex. Some celebrities make a career out of scandal. But more often, behind each scandal there is a politician, public servant or employee who finds their career has come to a sudden and dramatic finale. With less drama, there are many professionals who find their professional career derailed by a lapse.

Professional guard covers a multitude of sins, all of which are avoidable. It is a mindset which is inherently cautious and thinks ahead: "what is the worst thing that could happen if I do this . . .". Most traps are obvious and avoidable: you can identify most by thinking through some of the career disasters you have observed in your colleagues.

Here are a few of the more obvious elements of professional guard.

- Assume any email you send will be copied to the one person who you least want to see it. You will find this forces you to be naturally positive and action-focused: bitchiness is not good.
- Assume anything you say will be distorted and used as evidence against you. As with emails,

this means that the safe route is to be positive all the time.

- Assume that the person next to you on the plane or train works for your competitor: treat your paperwork, computer and phone conversations accordingly.
- The Christmas party and annual conference are a great opportunity to get drunk, flirt with the boss, photocopy your backside and screw up.
- How will your expenses claim look when the auditors select it for examination?
- How will the wonderful reward trip/junket look like when pictures turn up in the local or national newspapers?
- Do you really need to embellish your CV? Will that excuse for not turning up or being late hold up? If you are found out, you are dead meat. Honesty pays.

THE DAILY SKILLS OF MANAGEMENT

CHAPTER 29

THE DAILY SKILLS OF MANAGEMENT

If you can master
these basics,

YOU

will stand out
from your peers

Try explaining your job to a 3-year-old. The chances are that the intricacies of balancing budgets, managing projects and dealing with the politics of business life will be lost on the child. But if you explain that you spend most of the day talking, listening, reading, writing and meeting people, then even a 3-year-old might understand. And that is the essence of what managers do all day: we focus on basic tasks that even a 3-year-old can understand.

Because these tasks are so basic, we assume that we know how to do them well. Like breathing, it is assumed. But if you wanted to become a Buddhist monk you would spend your entire life mastering the art of breathing. Basic skills can be taken to great heights. Fortunately, you are unlikely to become a Buddhist monk while at work, so mastering the art of breathing is not essential to your success. But mastering the arts of reading, writing, talking, listening and meeting are essential. If you can master these basics, you will stand out from your peers who think that working on such basics is beneath their dignity.

Of course, you may think you can read, write, talk, listen and meet well. Now think of your colleagues. How many verbose reports do they write?

How often do they not appear to read and understand the beautifully crafted report you wrote? Do they bore you to tears with their presentations while they never seem to appreciate your brilliant and insightful presentation? You have plenty of evidence that other managers have not mastered the basics. And if we are humble, we have to admit that, from their perspective, we are part of the "other" managers who have not mastered the basics.

CHAPTER 30

MANAGE TIME EFFECTIVELY

The most valuable resource you can manage is your own time: we all have a sell-by date we cannot cheat. You have two ways of making the most of your time. You can be time efficient, which is maximising the amount of your activity. And you can be time efficient, which is about making sure you do the right things. Most time management is focused on efficiency. But if you are working very hard doing the wrong thing, then your time efficiency is 100% useless. Time management starts with effectiveness: doing the right thing.

As an exercise, try remembering what was special about ten years ago. Now try thinking how you want to remember this year ten or twenty years from now. You will not remember any year for the amount you beat budget by; you probably will not remember your precise income, or the number of emails you sent. Within your work environment there are plenty of things you have to do to just keep up: meetings, reports, expense claims, dealing with all the day-to-day noise of business life. But there are probably only one or two things that will make a difference to your career: opportunities to make a mark, build some skills and prove your worth. This is where your focus should be.

This is the essence of MBO – management by objectives. Set yourself some very clear objectives for the year. Some of them will be performance goals, others will be personal development goals. Once you have your goals for the year, start working back from the end of the year. What do you need to have achieved at the end of six months, at the end of this month, this week and today? You will lose some time to the noise of management, but do not let yourself be deafened by the daily noise of management. Keep focused on your goals and make sure you progress towards them. Once a week, take stock of how you are doing. Even if all you do is have one critical conversation with HR about the sorts of openings which are coming up, that may be enough to make the progress you require.

Unlike most human beings, managers are in the lucky position where they can manufacture more time. This unlikely breach of the laws of physics is made possible by the fact you do not have to do everything yourself. A good manager will delegate effectively and co-opt the support of other departments and colleagues to make things happen. The manager who bravely tries to do it all alone is a fool, not a hero.

In summary:

- Focus on the right goals uses time well; focus on the wrong goals is total waste of time
- Making progress against your goals is different from dealing with the daily grind of business as usual
- Be clear about your personal and professional goals
- Focus your efforts on your main goals and monitor your progress each week
- Create time by delegating work and enlisting the support of others

Remember the fable of the tortoise and the hare. The hare runs fast but runs in circles and gets nowhere. The tortoise is slow but makes steady progress. It's not how fast you run that counts, but where you run: achievement, not activity, matters.

CHAPTER 31

MANAGE TIME EFFICIENTLY

There are plenty of time management courses which will help you use time better. To help you save time by not going on them, here are the basics that you will learn on such a course.

1. *Only handle each piece of paper, email or report once.* You have four options with each one:
   - Ditch it: throw it in the number one file – junk
   - Delegate it: ask someone else to handle it
   - Do it: take action yourself
   - The last D is deadly: delay – this makes you look unprofessional, you waste time explaining the delay and life will have moved on without your input or influence.
2. *Do it right first time.* One of the biggest waste of management time and effort is re-work. You waste time doing the work again, and you waste more time defending the original work and arguing over changes.
3. *Avoid displacement activity.* The internet, thinking about things, filling in expense forms, chatting to colleagues and getting a cup of coffee are all wonderful ways of avoiding work. Displacement activity normally occurs when

you face a task that seems too large or too difficult: you have to cold call 50 clients, but you really do not want to. Deal with this through short interval scheduling: do not attempt to do the whole task at once. Break it down into bite-sized chunks and then promise yourself a small reward when you complete the small task. Perhaps set the goal of cold calling five clients, and then give yourself a deserved cup of coffee: if you are going to have displacement activity, make it work for you.

4. *Avoid the time thieves.* Queues, delays and public transport were not invented to frustrate you: they were invented to let you catch up with email, return phone calls and deal with the noise and grind of management.

5. *Manage your diary.* A diary packed with meetings is not necessarily a good diary. Are the meetings ones that get you closer to your goals, or are they responding to other people's agendas and needs? Where possible, schedule meetings for your convenience, not the convenience of others. Minimise the down time and disruption caused to your schedule by working to other people's timetables.

6. *Manage expectations.* If you have been asked to complete a task, be clear about when you can deliver it and what support you may need. Make sure you have properly understood the expectations and check in at key milestones to make sure you are on track: minimise the risk of re-work.

CHAPTER 32

HOW TO READ

You are reading this, so why on earth do you need to learn how to read? Because reading for business is different from reading for pleasure.

Reading for pleasure is, hopefully, a journey of discovery: you are led by the writer. In business, you do not want to be led by the writer. That is passive reading, and managers do not succeed by being passive. You need to read actively. Active reading requires some very simple preparation before you read anything.

Before you read any report, form your own point of view on two things:

1. What is your point of view on the subject? Do not get caught in the brilliant internal logic of the report in front of you. Form your own view. If the report says something different from what you expected, you will start to read much more critically. At the end, you will have a much better understanding about the arguments and issues, and you can choose intelligently to agree or disagree with the report.

2. Make a quick note of the key topics you expect to see covered in the report. This will help you spot the impossible and see the invisible: you

will see what is missing from the report. Again, this will help you read much more critically.

This is a basic discipline which works not just for reading but for meetings and for presentations. Do not listen passively to what is being said. Before the presentation or meeting starts remember the simple disciplines:

- Form your own point of view about the topic to be discussed
- Note what topics you expect to be covered

These disciplines convert you from a passive spectator to an active player. You will find you more easily come up with acute questions and insights. And eventually you will find that preparation only takes one, or at most two, minutes of your time, and can be done as you walk to the meeting. You will stand out from your more passive peers.

Read actively: read with prejudice and a point of view.

CHAPTER 33

HOW TO WRITE

GOOD WRITING IS A SIGN OF GOOD THINKING

As with reading, so with writing. Writing for business is different from writing for pleasure. And that does not mean filling documents with jargon in the hope of impressing people. Good writing is a sign of good thinking, so it pays to write well.

You do not need to be Shakespeare to write a good report. You need to follow five simple rules of editing:

1. *Write for the reader.* Work out why you are writing something and what your reader needs to know. This will help focus your document and reduce its size.
2. *Tell a story.* Ideally your document will be based on one simple idea. Often this can take the form of "here is the situation (or problem/ opportunity) and this is what we should do about it".
3. *Keep it short and simple.* It is easy to write long, hard to write short. Brevity forces clarity of thinking. A good document is not complete when you can say no more: it is complete when you can say no less. Keep cutting until you are left with the core of your thinking.
4. *Make it positive.* Readers do not want to hear what cannot be done: they want to know what

can be done. Avoid the passive tense and the impersonal. You may think it sounds serious and impressive. It is not. It is boring.

5. *Support assertions with facts.* If you say that something is strategic or important, that is simply your opinion. Show why it is so. And check all your facts: one bad fact undermines the credibility of your entire effort.

Keep yourself honest: get feedback on your work. Use a professional editor if you can. Once you have got past the personal affront of someone criticising your writing, you normally find that you improve your work.

Finally, avoid email hell. When you write any email assume that the one person you least want to see the email sees it. The way corporate life works, they probably will see it. This discipline forces you to be positive and results-focused, and helps you avoid the fallout.

CHAPTER 34

HOW TO LISTEN

The best leaders and the best salespeople have two ears and one mouth, and they use them in that proportion. They listen much more than they talk. There are good reasons why listening works:

■ You gather intelligence, so that when you choose to speak you can pitch your idea in the language that the other person wants to hear.
■ You build rapport. The sweetest sound in the world is, for many people, their own voice. If they find that you are ready to listen to their insight and views of the world, you make them feel good about themselves and about you.
■ You create the chance that they may listen to you. People are rarely ready to listen until they have been heard.

If this sounds obvious, look at what happens when you do not listen, instead you simply start pitching your latest and greatest idea:

■ You may speaking to the wrong person.
■ You may be speaking to the right person, but they have a completely different perspective or set of priorities which you do not know about. Without realising it, you may be putting your

foot in your mouth and shooting it: that is enter-
taining more than it is effective.

■ You disrespect the listener: you give them no
space to say their piece, and they will resent
this.

So how do you listen well?

The most important art to learn is paraphrasing.
When someone has been saying something, summarise it in your own words. This achieves three
things:

■ It confirms that you have understood properly
■ It helps you remember what has been said
■ It makes the other person shut up, or at least
move on

You have probably been in meetings where one
person is like a dog with a bone: they will not let
go of a point that they keep on making in the hope
that repetition will make it true. Everyone tries to
shut them up, but this simply makes the speaker
more determined to make their point. Instead of
shutting them up, try paraphrasing what they are
saying in a full and neutral way. It works like magic.
The speaker finally realises that they have been

heard and recognised, so they and the meeting can move on.

The second simple discipline is to debrief immediately after any significant meeting. You will have heard and seen things that your colleagues have not. You will have seen how a key executive reacted to a comment, and might have picked up a hint that the others have missed. Equally, it is just possible that your colleagues picked up things which you missed. Between you, you will have heard and seen more than you thought.

CHAPTER 35

HOW TO TALK

We all know how to talk. Talking to a big meeting turns some people into quivering wrecks, but the big meeting is where the big bosses will form their opinion about you. As with most management disciplines, practice makes perfect. But there are three consistent principles to observe that will make you a better presenter:

- Enthusiasm
- Expertise
- Empathy

Enthusiasm

If you are not enthusiastic, no one is going to be enthusiastic for you. So dare to be enthusiastic. Enthusiasm is not a certifiable disease: even in the most reserved organisation, enthusiasm is like a dose of fresh air.

Long after you have finished your presentation, people will have forgotten what you said. But they will not forget how you appeared. Do you want to be remembered as dull, boring and cynical or as being positive, energetic and enthusiastic?

Expertise

If you have been asked to speak on a topic, it is probably because you are seen to be the expert on it. Even the CEO will want to hear what you have to say: in your area of expertise you know more than the CEO. Rehearse your presentation. A good way to structure it is as follows:

■ Have a good start. Script your opening so that however nervous you may feel, you have a clear and confident start to get going.
■ Find some choice and memorable phrases which can act as way markers on your presentation.
■ Script a finish, so that you do not finish with the limp "any questions?"

Empathy

Before you talk you have to answer three questions:

1. *Who am I talking to?* In an audience of 100 people there may only be one or two people you want to impress or convince. Focus your talk on

those two people. The other 98 will not feel disenfranchised: they will enjoy a presentation which is unusually tight and has a focused logic with one clear argument.

2. *What do they need to hear?* See the world through their eyes. Do not say what you want to say; say what they need to hear and gear your argument to their expectations. If you know they have some concerns and objections, address them before they can raise the concerns themselves.

3. *Why should they listen to me?* Establish at the start of your objective the experience and knowledge you will draw on.

CHAPTER 36

THE ART OF A GOOD MEETING

IF YOU DON'T KNOW WHO THE FALL GUY IS, YOU ARE

Traders on Wall Street say that "if you don't know who the fall guy is, you are". That is a good motto for meetings. If you do not know what your objective is, be prepared to be disappointed. And in practice, never hold a meeting to make a decision: there is a danger that it will be the wrong one.

For every meeting you should know beforehand the outcome you want. And you should have done enough homework beforehand to be sure that you can achieve your outcome. A public setback is very hard to turn around later. Any decision that appears to be made in the meeting should simply be a public confirmation of the private agreements you have brokered in beforehand.

But you do not always need to go to a meeting for a decision. A good meeting will answer four questions positively for each attendee:

1. *What will I/we do differently* as a result of this meeting? This is normally the result of decisions being made. If you see an agenda item which looks like it might go the wrong way for you, do not fight the battle in the meeting. Fight it in private beforehand.
2. *What progress have I made* on my personal agendas at this meeting? The informal agenda

can be as useful as the formal agenda. Use the few minutes before and after a meeting to work your personal agenda with any hard-to-get executives you need to talk to. If necessary, simply set up a meeting with them for later.

3. *What did I learn* at this meeting? Meetings are a good way of gathering intelligence about people and priorities. If you go to a client meeting with a colleague, always debrief together immediately afterwards so that you can maximise your combined learning from the meeting.

4. *What did I contribute?* If you have nothing to contribute, do not go. Just because senior executives are there, avoid the temptation for "face time". If you are like a good child and you are seen, not heard, you will be treated like a child: you will be an irrelevance.

If you are calling a meeting, these four questions will help you decide who should attend. The larger the group, the less it is about making decisions and the more it is about communicating decisions. Equally, if you are invited to a meeting, use the four questions above to decide if you need or want to go to the meeting.

Many meetings are held simply because they are always held. These routine reporting meetings may be routine, but they still need to be planned. Make sure you understand the priorities and perspectives of senior colleagues who may be attending: avoid being surprised when they raise an unexpected point. Surprises are rarely good.

CHAPTER 37

THE USE AND ABUSE OF POWERPOINT

PowerPoint is a good example of how technology is only as good as the people who use it. In the wrong hands, PowerPoint is a giant leap backwards for mankind. Too many managers have had to suffer at the hands of the important panjandrum with nothing to say, or at the hands of the frenetic manager who has too much to say, and is determined to read his entire 300-page presentation verbatim.

Just because the technology allows us to produce 300-page presentations, it does not follow that we should. Just because we can produce fancy graphics, it does not mean that they will help with the clarity of communication.

The first rule of using PowerPoint is: don't use it. How many Presidents and Prime Ministers sit down to discuss the future of the world over competing PowerPoint presentations? Senior people do not hide behind PowerPoint: they talk face-to-face and use reason, not fancy slides. If you want to be treated as a junior person, then PowerPoint is a good way of going about it: you become the entertainment for the senior executives who will sit in judgement over you: you are far better off engaging them directly in conversation.

Your best visual aid is a blank sheet of paper. On it, be prepared to draw the key diagram or chart which makes your case: be sure to sit next to the person you want to influence so they are pulled into your act of drawing. As you both talk you can adjust your argument and your picture instead of ploughing on with a PowerPoint presentation which may be heading in the wrong direction. Peers talk to each other, they do not present at each other.

But there are occasions when you have to use PowerPoint. If you are addressing a very large group, some PowerPoint can help your audience see where you are. But remember that all the great orators of the past, like Churchill and Martin Luther King, did not need PowerPoint to hold their audience. If you are good at speaking, PowerPoint simply distracts from the star of the show: you.

If you must use PowerPoint, then use the rules of writing to prepare the presentation, and the rules of presentation to make the presentation.

There is one rule peculiar to PowerPoint: smart presenter, dumb slides. That means you should keep your slides to a minimum and each slide should be very simple. The slide should only capture the headline, not the detail, of what you intend to say. As the speaker, you can then be smart and illuminate the slide with your insight.

The cardinal sin of PowerPoint is to have smart slides and a dumb presenter. This occurs when the presenter puts everything that needs to be said on the slide and then proceeds to talk at the slides, reading out each one in full. The audience can read faster than the presenter can speak, and the presenter will be adding no value to the slides at all. It is a good way to bore and anger your audience, but not a good way to progress your career.

CHAPTER 38

PREPARING SPREADSHEETS

It is easy to
make things
complicated.

It takes genius to
make them
simple.

There are three rules for spreadsheets:

- Keep it simple
- The spreadsheet is only as good as the person behind it
- It's not the numbers that count: it's the assumptions

Follow these three assumptions, and you have a chance of producing a spreadsheet which is convincing. Analysts think that spreadsheets do analysis. For managers, spreadsheets are about persuasion, not analysis. That changes everything.

Keep it simple

It is easy to make things complicated. It takes genius to make them simple. Think of $e = mc^2$ – simple, but devastating.

The more complicated a spreadsheet becomes, the less anyone can understand it. It also becomes harder to change in response to the inevitable requests for changes, and it becomes easier to make mistakes which are harder to track down. And people tend not to trust things they do not understand. So you may impress yourself with your brilliant spreadsheet, but it serves no purpose unless it can communicate and convince.

If you have to have a complicated spreadsheet, put a summary at the front of not more than twenty lines and ten columns. This should be where anyone else can enter some key variables, do some "what if" calculations and see the result on the same page. Simplicity and clarity are more convincing than complexity.

The spreadsheet is only as good as the person behind it

Venture capitalists are routinely presented with business plans that promise the earth but are more likely to turn to dust. The spreadsheet always looks brilliant, however marginal the business plan may be in reality.

The quickest way to see past the spreadsheet is to look at the person behind it. If you have a great track record, you will be believed. If you have not yet got a track record with the person who you need to persuade, find someone who does have a good track record. Get them to support and endorse your spreadsheet.

It's not the numbers that count: it's the assumptions

Most spreadsheets are constructed from the bottom right corner backwards: start with the desired answer and then work the assumptions to make sure you get the answer you want.

So no one should believe the spreadsheet presented to them: of course the answer will look attractive. Whether the assumptions that lie behind the answer are any good is the real question. Start with the big assumptions and the golden numbers.

The big assumptions are items such as market size, market growth, number of employees and cost per employee. Do not worry about the cost of buying the coffee maker, unless you are in the coffee maker business.

The golden numbers are numbers which are at the heart of your business. Different industries and departments have different measures of productivity and performance. Test the spreadsheet against the golden numbers for your part of the business. If the number does not look right, it is not right.

Ultimately, spreadsheets are not about the quality of the maths: they are about the quality of the thinking.

MANAGE YOUR CAREER

CHAPTER 39

MANAGE YOUR CAREER

A good manager will learn to manage people, budgets, tasks, customers, technology, change, finance and much else besides. But the most important thing any manager has to manage is his or her own career. Unlike all the other skills of management, there are no second chances in career management. If you mess up a project, you can always apply your learning to the next one. If you mess up your career, you have messed up your career. You always have the option of rediscovering that long-lost dream of working on a vegan commune, but that is probably not the ambition that you have today.

In theory, your boss and your firm should take an active interest in your career and do the right thing for you. In theory, there should not be war, famine or accordion players on the Underground. In practice, your boss has other things to worry about. Your HR department will want to help you, and a few hundred of your closest colleagues and competitors for promotion.

The only person who really cares about your career is yourself. It is very hard to get impartial advice about what to do next. And inevitably, your circumstances are going to be unique.

In the past, career management was pretty simple for managers. You joined a firm, and forty years later you were given a carriage clock before disappearing to play bridge and die. In between, the personnel department would do what today's Strategic Human Capital Division does: they would guide your career in a direction deemed to be good for the firm and, possibly, for you.

Today, managers suffer the curse of freedom. We can choose our own destiny, but equally we are responsible for our destiny. So for many managers career is no longer a noun: it is a verb which describes how we career from triumph to disaster and back again.

With freedom comes responsibility. We can no longer rely on a paternalistic life-time employer to look after us. We make our own luck. If we have a lousy firm, a lousy boss and a lousy job we have only ourselves to blame. And only we can remedy the situation. Complaining about a lousy firm, boss and job is a popular but pointless pastime.

But through this fog of confusion you can find a few basic principles to guide you. This section of the book outlines the rules for managing the most important thing you can manage: your career.

CHAPTER 40

THE MANAGEMENT JOURNEY

HOW CAN A PROMOTION BE A CRISIS?

Most career people start by learning a craft: teaching, accounting, analysis, trading or an arcane craft like settlements in the tripartite asset collaterised repo market. If you master these skills well, you will be promoted and face your first great career crisis.

How can a promotion be a crisis? The problems start if you fail to recognise that the rules of the game have changed: you cannot do more of the same if you want to succeed. You face the problem of the leader in the locker room. Imagine you are a very good football player. You get asked to manage the team. As a role model for the team you train and play harder than ever: you make every tackle, every pass and every shot you can. And you fail. Because as manager your job is not to make all the tackles, shots and passes. Your job is to select the right team, train them, motivate them, make sure they work together in the right positions and prepare them for the competition.

In the same way, a manager is not meant to do the job of the people he or she manages. The manager has to select the right team, train them, motivate them and make sure they work together in the right positions. The manager has to learn a completely new set of skills than the successful player.

As your career progresses, so your skill set will shift from technical skills to people and political skills. If you cannot manage people and politics you will not progress far, even though you may make a good living out of being a technical expert.

With this in mind, it makes sense to start building people and political skills as early as you can. And if you work in a professional services firm, you need to master the management of clients. Managing client projects is simple: managing the relationship, building and extending the relationship is the core of what partners do. If you get the chance to try these skills on a client that is too small for the partners to bother with, take your chance.

Building people, political and possibly client management skills should be your guiding light in deciding which assignments to take on and which to duck.

CHAPTER 41

WHAT IT TAKES TO GET AHEAD

Most management gurus tell you half the truth, at best, about what it takes to become an outstanding manager.

They will tell you about the need for vision, handling people, dealing with crises and all the other good stuff that makes up the corporate speaking circuit. Here are seven vital qualities you are less likely to hear them talk about:

1. *Be ambitious for your organisation and yourself.* Stretch yourself and your team to achieve more than ever; keep on learning and growing. Don't accept excuses, don't be a victim: take responsibility.
2. *Work the politics.* Find the right assignments, right support and right mentors. Set expectations well. Negotiate budgets hard. Wake up to the reality of corporate life.
3. *Stay positive, stay motivated.* Even when you are dealing with surly customers, sneaky colleagues, aggressive bosses and unhelpful staff, learn to wear the mask: stay calm and be positive. The moment you descend to their level, you lose.

4. *Working in vehicles.* If you cannot work in taxis, trains and planes, you will waste more time than you can afford. Staring out of the window mindlessly is not good.

5. *Dieting.* Managers are surrounded by biscuits, cookies and other corporate death food; and then there are the inevitable lunches, dinners and hotel breakfasts. Either learn to love the fruit, or start jogging. Or die early as an obese alcoholic. But to this day, some firms demand that you put your liver on the line: if you do not drink and entertain, you fail. Pick your diet to fit your firm.

6. *Sleeping on planes and dealing with jet lag.* In any large organisation, a manager who is going places will go to many places: you will spend a large amount of time on planes. Business class is not for fancy meals and watching movies: it is for work or sleep.

7. *Ruthless time management.* Queues were invented to let leaders catch up with emails and phone calls; ditch or delegate everything you can; fix appointments around your diary, not around other people's. One of the joys of top management is that you will never suffer the

rush hour. You will arrive before it and leave after it. Make time work for you.

These seven qualities add up to a person who is pretty driven: they are often not comfortable people to be with. Not surprisingly, many people prefer to keep their humanity and their life than make the sacrifices to get to the top. You choose.

CHAPTER 42

HOW TO GET PROMOTED

In the old days, you worked hard, kept your nose clean and waited for your turn to take a step up the career ladder. Only the most naïve manager would rely on that formula today. The new rules of management mean that you have to manage your promotion prospects actively.

Think about promotion from the perspective of the people who are deciding on promotions. If you ever sit on a promotions commission, you will find yourself presented with bundles of promotion packages. Each one is a eulogy to the individual in question. This is your boss doing your best for you. You will be lavished with praise, such that you appear to have single-handedly transformed the entire firm. And that is the problem: every package says the same thing. So the packages are not credible and there is no way of distinguishing between candidates.

So you need to stand out. You have three ways of doing this.

1. *Build a claim to fame.* You need to have some stand-out achievement. It is not enough to have beaten budget and shown great personal skills: everyone else will be able to make the same claim. You need to have sorted out a crisis, led

some landmark initiative, done something that makes people take notice.

2. *Make moments of truth work for you.* There are set piece events where you are on display to top management: this is where they will form their opinions. So if you have a speech or a presentation to make, overinvest in it. If you need to get a speech coach, get one. Appearances count.

3. *Build the right image.* Even if top bosses are not familiar with the details of what you have really achieved, they will be familiar with you as a person. If you are always positive, volunteering to help out and action-focused you will do far better than the technically excellent colleague who is always a bit dour, cautious and occasionally cynical. You cannot fake this. But you can work in places that bring out the best in you, and you can focus on always presenting your best face to the firm.

CHAPTER 43

HOW NOT TO
GET PROMOTED

TOP MANAGEMENT IS FAR EASIER AND MORE REWARDING THAN MIDDLE MANAGEMENT

Leading from the middle is the hardest stage of any manager's career. Whisper it quietly, but top management is far easier and more rewarding than middle management. At the top you have more control over your destiny, and more resources at your disposal.

Many people never make it out of the matrix in the middle of most organisations. Here are the five most common types of career hold up:

1. *The boy scout*, who believes that working hard and honestly will get you to the top. No, it will not. You need a claim to fame, to stake your claim and to have sponsors who will look out for you at promotion, bonus and assignment time.

2. *The expert*, who gets promoted on the basis of deep functional expertise. These people are good at managing ideas, techniques. Think accountants, lawyers, IT specialists. They fail to learn the top management skills of managing people, politics and business.

3. *The politician*, who is the opposite of the boy scout. Politicians always associate themselves with success. They vanish when there is trouble. They plot and connive. They can go far, but

most get caught in the end: their enemies mul-
tiply over the years and eventually people notice
that the politicians have not actually achieved
anything.

4. *The autocrat*, who acts like they already are
top managers. Their version of being a team
player is "play my way or you are not a team
player". Again, they can go far, but they are
often highly divisive. Like the politician, they
acquire enemies who are only too happy to stick
the knife in as soon as the autocrat has an inevitable setback.

5. *The cave dweller.* Most large organisations
have functional silos and layers like a pancake.
When you cross a silo with a pancake you get
a cave: this is where some middle managers
hide. They protect their little piece of territory,
to recreate the certainty they enjoyed in junior
management. They fail to work with the complexity, ambiguity and opportunity offered by
large organisations.

So how do you get through the middle management minefield? Successful middle managers all
have elements, but not excess, of the boy scout
(hard work), the politician (understand the organi-

sation) and the autocrat (make things happen). Most, but not all, are very good at working with people.

Inevitably, the skills that leaders really need to learn are ones for which there is precious little training. You have to discover the skills and the rules of the game yourself.

CHAPTER 44

HOW TO GET FIRED

There are plenty of creative ways of getting fired. At the extremes, theft, illegal conduct and a Christmas party which gets out of hand are some of the more creative and unusual ways of finding the exit door.

But normally, most firms and most bosses are quite reluctant to fire people. The firm fears litigation. And most bosses, apart from a few psychopaths, are mortified at the prospect of firing anyone, let alone a colleague they know. Of course, if you have a gold medal in incompetence, then eventually nothing can save you. In some firms and some parts of the public sector you are more likely to die in service than be fired for cause; and these are not physically dangerous occupations.

Bosses forgive most sins, but there is one sin which is unforgivable: disloyalty. You have to be able to trust your boss and your boss has to trust you. Once that bond of trust is broken there is normally no going back. It may take a few weeks or a few months, but usually you will find that you and your boss part ways. If you are disloyal once, you will move within the firm. Once you establish a reputation for disloyalty, no one will want you on their team. You will find yourself looking elsewhere.

Disloyalty is not just about trying to stab the boss in their back. It can be as simple as not speaking up for the boss, or even disagreeing, in a big meeting. Or it can be trying to delegate the blame upwards when things go wrong. Or hiding bad news which the boss only finds out about when meeting the CEO: you have just made your boss look like an idiot in front of the CEO and that is not good for either of your careers.

You do not have to be a yes-man. You can build credibility and trust by disagreeing with the boss and having that difficult conversation, as long as it is in private. In public, you have to be a united team.

CHAPTER 45

WHEN TO MOVE ON

IT IS GREENEST WHERE IT RAINS THE MOST

From time to time, headhunters may call you, promising greener pastures elsewhere. Gently remind them that it is greenest where it rains the most. Other firms look better from the outside, but will suffer the same challenges your firm faces.

There are several bad reasons for moving:

- You do not like your boss. Most people do not leave their firm; they leave their boss. This is a mistake. The corporate carousel keeps on turning and no boss is for ever: you or the boss is likely to move within 18 months. And the same goes for the firm you are thinking about joining. The great new boss you are excited about working with will soon move on, and your next boss could be the boss from hell.
- You can get a 10% pay rise. This is a small bribe which is not worth it. Focus on what you can be earning in five years' time, not next year. Build your skills and experience, and the performance and pay will follow.
- You can get a 100% pay rise. This is incredibly attractive and dangerous. Beware the forces of hedonic adaptation: you and your family will quickly get used to the champagne lifestyle. Going back to the beer and sandwiches way of

living will seem impossible. So you will be trapped and will have to do whatever it takes to survive in your new role, even if you find you hate the job, you compromise your ethics and have to work all hours.

Then there are some good reasons for moving:

- You get up in the morning and your heart sinks at the prospect of going into work again. You cannot succeed at something you dislike. Move on.
- You are not getting the right skills and experience: your career is going nowhere. It is very easy to get trapped in a specialist niche at work, where you become the great expert. The firm will love you for it and will want to keep you in your expert role. If that is what you want, fine. If you want to build and grow your career, you have to make sure you are getting the right experiences. If your firm will not do that for you, find one that will.
- You are about to be fired. It is far easier to get a new job while you still have a job. Once you leave, even for good reasons, any prospective employer may suspect that you are damaged

goods. Meanwhile, your existing employer will be only too pleased to ease your passage into other employment without going through all the grief of forcing you out.

Finally, when you move, do it well. Never bad mouth your existing or previous employers. Prospective employers get turned off by that sort of behaviour: it shows that you are negative, disloyal and untrustworthy. They will wonder what you say about them behind their backs. And since most people move within an industry, you will find that years later your comments and reputation will catch up with you, not to your advantage. Find the positives from your last role, and find positive reasons for moving, such as building your experience and getting the right sort of role.

CHAPTER 46

FIND THE RIGHT BOSS

Many managers believe that the boss they work for is the product of a completely random set of events which the HR department is somehow involved in. This is a disaster. Your boss is the single most important influence on your career.

A good and strong boss will help you levitate magically through the firm: you rise mysteriously on his or her coat tails. A bad and weak boss is likely to hide their incompetence by firing you. Your boss will lead you on the road to heaven or hell: it pays to make sure you have the right boss going in the right direction.

You cannot guarantee the boss you get, but you can load the dice in your favour. Here's how.

1. *Build your network.* Your network should tell you who are the good bosses and who are the death star bosses. And it should also tell you what openings are arising. If a death star boss is looking for victims to work on a team, make sure that you are very, very busy elsewhere. Be unavailable. If a great boss is looking for new team members, it does no harm to make your interest known and make it clear that you could be available. Make yourself known to good bosses, perhaps by helping them in a small

way: bosses always like to recruit people they know than to rely on the vagaries of the HR system.

2. *Find a sponsor.* A sponsor is someone who is at least two levels above you in the firm, and who takes a positive interest in you and your career. These people get early sight of threats and opportunities, can manage politics for you and give you useful advice on dealing with top management. The deal with a sponsor is simple. The sponsor likes to have some eyes and ears lower in the organisation; appreciates someone who can put in some voluntary effort on new ideas and likes to be flattered by offering the wisdom of their experience. Most managers do not seek sponsors, so the field is open to you.

3. *Be loyal.* Once you find a good boss, hang on to him or her. A boss who is successful, looks after you and you like working for is like gold dust. Even the fattest such boss is worth more than their weight in gold for your future salary prospect. Most good bosses like to keep their "A" team around them as they progress. Make sure you are part of that core team. Put in the extra discretionary effort; be overtly loyal and supportive; be consistently positive; and always

deliver on commitments. In short, model management best practice.

Remember the dictum of Lord Palmerston, British Foreign Secretary at the time of Empire: "Nations have no permanent friends or allies: they only have permanent interests". No boss is for ever, and they are not your friend even if they invite you out to dinner. You will have common interests, but when those interests diverge then you will find your apparent friendship counts for nothing. The boss will look after his or her career, not yours, as the top priority. This means you should avoid becoming completely dependent on one boss. You need your network and you need your plan B.

CHAPTER 47

WHAT YOUR BOSS WANTS FROM YOU

A CAREER IS A MARATHON NOT A *SPRINT*

At one level it is obvious what your boss wants from you: this will be laid out in your budget, your personal development plan, your MBO for the year and all the other planning and control documents that underpin corporate life. You need to deliver against these expectations as best you can.

You will be judged not just on what you do, but on how you do it. I have asked thousands of bosses what they expect from their teams, and here is what they said:

■ Reliability
■ Ambition
■ Proactivity
■ Intelligence
■ Hard work

As you look at the list, you may think it is a very undemanding list. It is undemanding. Remarkably, bosses think that little more than half of their team members jump all these hurdles. So if you want to stand out relative to your peers you do not have to be a corporate gold medallist. Forget the hype about excellence. Success comes from being less incompetent and less idle than your colleagues.

This is what bosses meant when they picked the five words above.

Reliability. This is number one because bosses hate surprises. As a team member, that means you have to set expectations very clearly and very early. If you promise something, deliver. If you cannot deliver, then have the courage to say so before accepting the challenge. And if things start to go wrong, overcommunicate and communicate early.

Ambition. Bosses want ambitious staff with drive and energy who will go above and beyond the call of duty. Personal ambition goes hand-in-hand with ambition for the team: going for stretching goals and not accepting second best. This is better than having a team which lives in their comfort zone and does the minimum to get by.

Proactivity. Bosses need teams with initiative, who will make things happen. A team which is purely reactive and waits for instructions is a drain of energy and a waste of resources. So take the initiative and do not wait to be told what to do.

Intelligence. Bosses are not expecting you to be Einstein. But they are expecting common sense. That means they want you to handle day-to-day problems and challenges without delegating everything up to them to solve.

Hard work. Forget the myths about one-minute-managing and the four-hour work week. There are not many short cuts in a career, unless you marry a billionaire or set up Google. Success requires hard work. A career is a marathon, not a sprint. Most people fall by the wayside at some point: if you have the stamina to keep going, you will succeed.

CHAPTER 48

MANAGE YOUR BOSS

NEVER BECOME OVERDEPENDENT ON YOUR BOSS

Your boss is a wonderful opportunity to practise and develop your management and influencing skills. You probably see a lot of your boss, so you get a lot of practice time. You have no control over your boss, so you have to fine tune the influencing skills that you need to use on all your peers.

If you have a good boss, you will enjoy developing your management skills on him or her. But do not fall into the trap of assuming that, because you are friends, all will be well. Your boss may look out for your interests when times are good, but no boss will sacrifice their own interests or the interests of the firm at the expense of looking after you. This leads to the first rule of managing your boss: never become overdependent on your boss. Make sure you have a network of support across the firm, so that if your boss moves or hard times come, you have alternatives.

Having a bad boss is a wonderful opportunity to put your management skills to the acid test: if you can learn how to manage a bad boss, you can manage anyone. Even a bad boss, with all their failings, became a boss for some reason. Normally, they have at least one stand-out strength among their many weaknesses. Learn positively from their stand-out strength, and learn what not to do from their many failings. Either way, always learn by observing what your boss does.

Four principles lie at the heart of managing your boss well, and all have been covered so far. You need to bring them together for your boss:

1. Deliver on your formal commitments: budget, MBO, development plan as appropriate.
2. Adopt the behaviour of a good team member: reliability, ambition, proactivity, intelligence and hard work.
3. Build trust. Without trust, there is no relationship. Remember that trust has three elements:
   - Values alignment: always be loyal, sing the same tune as your boss
   - Credibility: always deliver, so manage expectations well
   - Manage risk: overcommunicate, flag bad news early, avoid surprises
4. Adapt your style to suit your boss. We have already seen in the styles of management how everyone is different and no one has the right style. But that is not quite true. In practice, your

boss has the "right" style, in the sense that you have to adapt your style because your boss won't adapt their style to yours.

If you can manage your boss well, you will have learned how to manage anyone well.

CHAPTER 49

FIND THE RIGHT ASSIGNMENT

As with bosses, there are death star assignments from which no career has ever been known to escape. It pays to avoid the corporate equivalent of cleaning toilets in Siberia. And then there are the dream assignments. The same rules apply as in finding the right boss:

- Build your network: get the intelligence on what opportunities are emerging
- Find a sponsor who can look out for your interests
- Do not leave assignments to the vagaries of the HR process: be active in managing your career.

This begs the question: what is the right assignment?

The right assignment is not necessarily the easiest or most enjoyable assignment. These are not the assignments where you learn the most or build the skills and experiences on which you depend.

To judge whether you are being offered the right assignment, ask the following questions:

- Will I develop the right skills for the future?
- How will this experience develop my profile within the firm?

- Is the project and role set up for success or failure?
- What will be my specific role and will it allow me to build a claim to fame?
- What opportunities are likely to emerge at the end of this assignment or is it a career dead end?
- Who will my boss be and am I happy working for that boss?
- Will I enjoy this assignment or not?

Inevitably, the answers to all these questions will not all point in the same direction. But you have a far better chance of making the right decision if you actively manage the process rather than waiting for HR to take care of your career and your life.

CHAPTER 50

MANAGEMENT OR LEADERSHIP?

What is the difference between management and leadership? Do not write your answers on both sides of the paper at the same time.

The simple answer is that leadership sells more books. People think leadership is more aspirational than management. That is a shame, because management is at least as important and in many ways it is more difficult than leadership.

Leaders may dream the dream, lead the revolution and change the world. But before and after the revolution you need cohorts of managers who know how to make the system work: they can make the trains run on time and ensure the rubbish is collected. For every inspiring leader, you need dozens of perspiring managers who convert the dream into reality. Managers are at least as important as leaders.

Management is also more difficult than leadership, especially in the middle of the organisation. Look at what happens in terms of power and ambiguity at different levels of the organisation:

New joiners, recent graduates. You probably have to work very hard to meet challenging goals. You do not have much power: you do as you are told. But what you lose in power, you make up for in clarity. At least there is no ambiguity about what you are meant to do, even if it is hard. At this level, you may experience pressure but you will not experience real stress. The difference between pressure and stress is control: when you have no control, then you feel stress. Because you have clarity about your goals, you are at least in control of your destiny.

Top leaders and managers. At the top you have all the power you lacked at the start of your career. It is possible your authority and responsibility finally come into balance. But what you gain in power, you lose in clarity. At the top, you have freedom but you also have the complexity of many competing stakeholders and goals which you need to balance. You start your career with low power and low ambiguity; you end it with high power and high ambiguity. By the time you finish, you are in high control and you will feel low stress: never believe the nonsense that is spouted about how hard it is at the top. It is far easier than being in the middle.

Managing in the middle. Middle management is the paranoia zone. Your responsibility exceeds your authority. You face huge ambiguity with competing pressures on your time; you have to work through people you do not control; you are coordinating a troupe of wildly divergent stakeholders and interests. Not surprisingly, many people burn out, stress out and drop out at this level. Only when you break through to top management does life become easier again.

Management may be hard, but if it was easy it would not be so rewarding. Enjoy the journey.